A QUESTION AND ANSWER STORYBOOK

Do the Doors Open by Magic?

and other supermarket questions

by Catherine Ripley

illustrated by Scot Ritchie

OWL BOOKS

Do the Doors Open by Magic? and other supermarket questions

Owl Books are published by Greey de Pencier Books Inc.,
179 John Street, Suite 500, Toronto, Ontario M5T 3G5

Owl and the Owl colophon are trademarks of Owl Communications.
Greey de Pencier Books Inc. is a licensed user of trademarks of Owl Communications.

Distributed in the United States by Firefly Books (U.S.) Inc.,
230 Fifth Avenue, Suite 1607, New York, NY 10001

This book was published with the generous support of the Canada Council, the Ontario Arts
Council, and the Government of Ontario through the Ontario Publishing Centre.

Special thanks to *Chickadee* Magazine for some great questions;
Marvin Jones, Coca-Cola Bottling; Jim LaMorre and staff, Loeb Club Plus, Manotick, Ontario;
Environment Canada; Kraft General Foods Canada Inc.; Sylvie Bertrand, Dr. Randall Brooks
and Dr. Helen Grave-Smith, National Museum of Science and Technology;
Ontario Arts Council; Gordon and Marion Penrose; Bruce Ripley; Sheba, Kat and Trudee for
their careful, friendly editing; Mary for making the the words and pictures work together;
Scot for his delightful illustrations; and my family for their love and patience.

DEDICATION

**For K. Green of Legal, Alberta, who sparked the series by writing
a letter to *Chickadee* Magazine, and for Sheba who fanned
the fire in my mind and kept it burning. Thank you.**

Canadian Cataloguing in Publication Data

Ripley, Catherine, 1957–

Do the doors open by magic? and other supermarket

questions

ISBN 1-895688-35-3 (bound). – ISBN 1-895688-40-X (pbk.)

1. Supermarkets - Juvenile literature. I. Ritchie,

Scot. II. Title.

HF5469.R56 1995   j381'.148   C94-932490-6

Design and Art Direction: Mary Opper

Also available:

Why is Soap so Slippery? and other bathtime questions

Printed in Hong Kong

A   B   C   D   E   F

Contents

Do the doors open by magic?

No — without knowing it, *you* open them! Above the door, a special electronic "eye" sends down an invisible beam that spreads out in front of the door. When you walk through the beam, you break it. That tells a motor near the doors to start working, and to open the doors for you.

Where do apples come from in winter?

Some come from where it's summer, very far away. Others come from huge storerooms filled with — zzzzz — sleeping apples. Even after they are picked, apples use a gas in the air called oxygen, along with light and warmth, to get riper. Back in the fall, some apples were shut inside huge rooms. The rooms were kept cold and dark, and a special machine removed most of the oxygen from the air. So, the apples fell asleep, and ripened very, very slowly. Months later, when workers took the apples out of the rooms to send to the store, they woke up fresh and crunchy.

Why does it smell so good here?

Because hot air rises. And there's a lot of hot air around when people are baking bread. Air rises inside the sticky bread dough as it bakes, making the bread light and fluffy. And some of the hot, steamy air rises out of the bread and floats through the air, right to your nose. The steam carries with it the smells of all the ingredients in the bread, mixed together to make that yummy bread smell. Once the baked goods are cooled and bagged, the air can't bring the smells to your nose as easily.

How does all this food get here?

In all kinds of trucks! Every day the supermarket manager orders food to sell at the store. Big transport trucks bring in the orders. Food that needs to be kept frozen or really cold comes in a truck that's like a giant freezer on wheels. Other refrigerated trucks are kept just cold enough to bring in milk and meat. Sometimes fresh-picked fruits and vegetables come from nearby farms in smaller pick-up trucks. And snack foods like potato chips come in their very own — you guessed it! — transport truck.

What's behind the big doors?

Lots! Everything that keeps the workers working, the shelves stocked, the freezers full, and the whole supermarket running is behind these doors. Turn the page to sneak a peek . . .

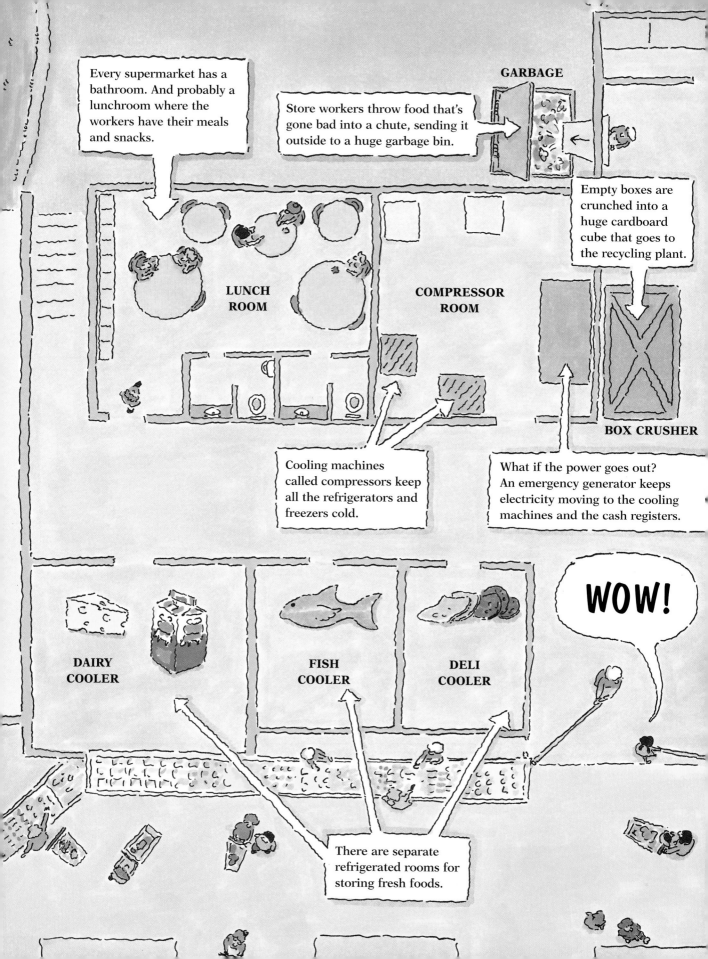

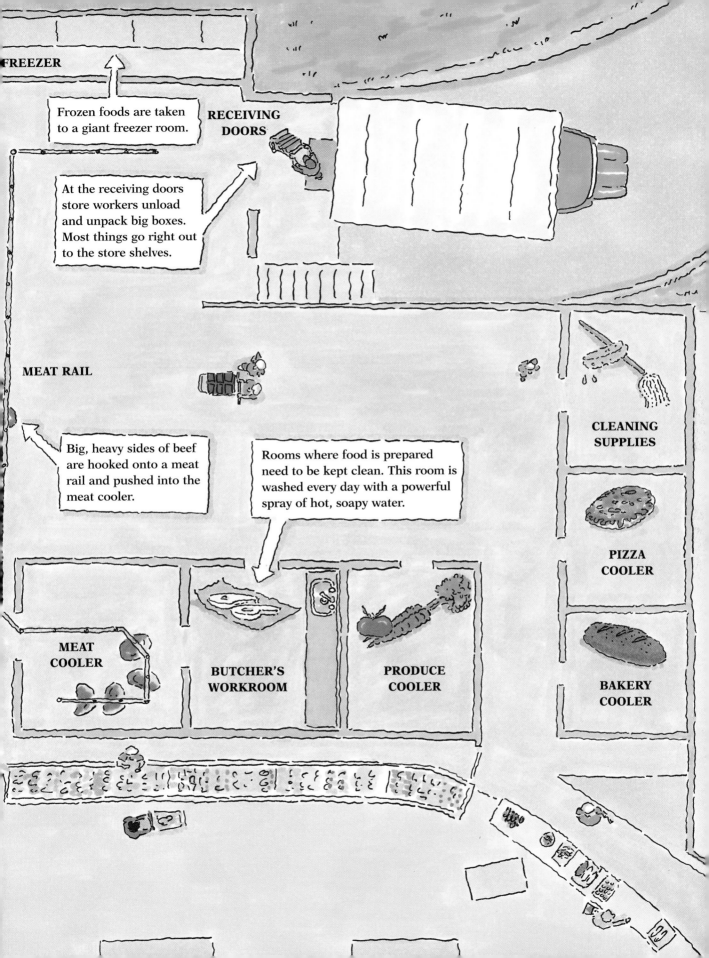

FREEZER

Frozen foods are taken to a giant freezer room.

RECEIVING DOORS

At the receiving doors store workers unload and unpack big boxes. Most things go right out to the store shelves.

MEAT RAIL

Big, heavy sides of beef are hooked onto a meat rail and pushed into the meat cooler.

Rooms where food is prepared need to be kept clean. This room is washed every day with a powerful spray of hot, soapy water.

CLEANING SUPPLIES

PIZZA COOLER

BAKERY COOLER

MEAT COOLER

BUTCHER'S WORKROOM

PRODUCE COOLER

What holds jelly dessert together?

Braids! But not the kind in your sister's hair — gelatin braids. Jelly powder contains gelatin that makes food thick and bouncy, plus sugar and other things to give it color and flavor. Bits of gelatin, so small you can't see them without a microscope, contain many tiny strands, like a braid. When boiling water dissolves the jelly powder, the gelatin braids come undone, and the strands get all mixed in with the water. Then, as the liquid cools, the gelatin pulls back together, trapping the water and sugar in between the strands. And that's what holds together this jiggly treat!

Why are some eggs brown and some white?

It depends on the type of chickens that laid them. White Leghorn chickens, for example, lay most of the white eggs that you can buy in a store. Brown eggs usually come from red hens. But there are all sorts of other chickens: some lay white eggs, some lay brown eggs, some lay speckled eggs, and the Ameraucana chicken from South America lays blue eggs!

How do they make spaghetti look like spaghetti and macaroni look like macaroni?

It's a story full of holes! In the noodle factory, the stiff pasta dough is pushed through holes in special metal plates. The shape of the pasta that comes out depends on the shape of the hole it was pushed through. When the dough is pushed through tiny holes, you get spaghetti. When it is pushed through round holes that have small pins in them, the dough comes out in long tubes. When the tubes are chopped into short pieces, you get macaroni.

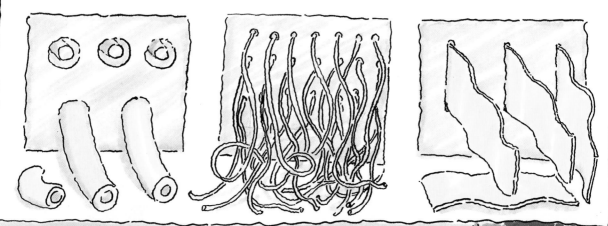

What puts the fizz in soda pop?

Thousands of tiny bubbles. Before soda pop is put in cans or bottles, it goes through a machine that makes it cold and presses on it. This makes it easy to fill the liquid with bubbles of a harmless gas called carbon dioxide. When you open a bottle or can of soda pop, the tiny bubbles begin to rush up to the top and burst. The fizz in your drink is lots of little bubbles bursting — pop, pop! Eventually all of the bubbles pop, and no more bubbles means no more fizz. Your soda pop has gone "flat."

Why do my fingers stick to the frozen juice cans?

Your fingers must be wet! When your fingers are even a little wet or sweaty and the cans are in a very, very cold freezer, you'll probably get stuck. As soon as you touch the can, the wetness on your skin freezes to the can, like an icy glue, and sticks your fingers to it. Brrrr!

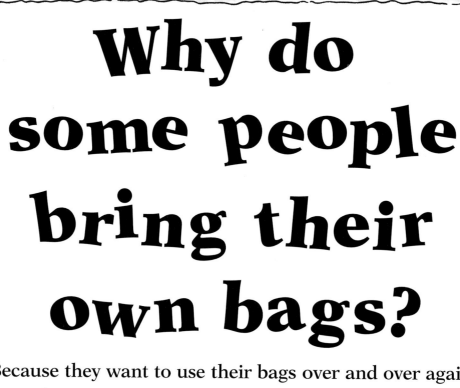

Why do some people bring their own bags?

Because they want to use their bags over and over again.
To make paper bags, you start by cutting down trees.
To make plastic bags, you start by drilling for petroleum underground. Then lots of electricity is needed to make the trees and petroleum into bags. If you only use the bags once, they end up in the garbage and you have to start again. But if you reuse your bags again and again, or if you carry cloth or string bags that last a very long time, you won't waste trees, petroleum or electricity. And you won't add to the garbage.

Supermarket Bits

If the store doors don't open automatically for your little brother, it's probably because he's too short! The beam from the electronic eye gets weaker and wider the further it goes. A very short person doesn't break the beam, so the motor doesn't start, and the doors don't open.

On most store items you'll find a Universal Product Code, or UPC. The bars and numbers are a code for the name and price of the product. If a store "scans" these bar codes into a computer, it gives you the information hidden in the codes. The information flashes on the cashier's screen, and then is printed on the cash register tape for you to take home.

Surprise . . . cheese comes from grass! Cows eat grass, and inside their bodies the grass gets turned into milk. After the cow is milked, some of the milk is used to make cheese. Ta-da — cheese from grass!